SUPER SPORTS

Water Sports

DAVID JEFFERIS

RAINTREE
STECK-VAUGHN
PUBLISHERS

A Harcourt Company

Austin   New York
www.raintreesteckvaughn.com

Published by Raintree Steck-Vaughn Publishers, an imprint of Steck-Vaughn Company

Library of Congress Cataloging-in-Publication Data

Jefferis, David.
    Water sports / David Jefferis.
       p. cm. -- (Super sports)
    Includes bibliographical references and index.
       ISBN 0-7398-4344-3
       1. Aquatic sports--Juvenile literature. [1. Aquatic sports] I. Title. II. Super sports (Austin, Tex.)

GV770.5 .J44 2001
797--dc21   2001016096

Acknowledgments
We wish to thank the following individuals and organizations for their help and assistance and for supplying material in their collections:
AllSport UK Ltd, Alpha Archive, Silvain Cazenave/Nikon, Club Med, Didier Givois, F. Monsis, Ker Robertson, Richard Martin, Stephen Munday, Matthieu Pendle, Loick Peyron, Philip Plisson, Ker Robertson, Pascal Rondeau, A. Sezerat, Sygma, Vandystadt Sports Photos, Nick Wilson, Yamaha, Y. Zedda

Diagrams by Gavin Page

Printed in China and bound in the United States.

1 2 3 4 5 6 7 05 04 03 02 01

▲ Hurtling down-river in a rubber raft can be an exciting ride! It's called white-water rafting, after the foam in the wildest parts of the river.

Contents

Look out for the Super Sports Symbol

Look for the yacht symbol in boxes like this.
Here you will find extra water sports facts, stories,
and useful tips for beginners.

World of Water Sports

▲ Being a good swimmer helps if you're interested in water sports, but you don't have to be a sports champion.

▼ A ski-boat needs a big engine. Learning to water ski is not difficult, but you must have a good sense of balance.

Power is needed for all water sports. The energy for one sport or another can come from the wind, a powerful engine, or your muscles!

The great thing about water sports is that you can have fun at almost any level. A trip to a swimming pool, canoeing, and sailing can be just as exciting as an expensive motorboat or an ocean-going yacht.

Safety is very important. So learn to swim well before trying the things in this book! Training is important, too. A good teacher will show you the basics of a sport quickly and safely.

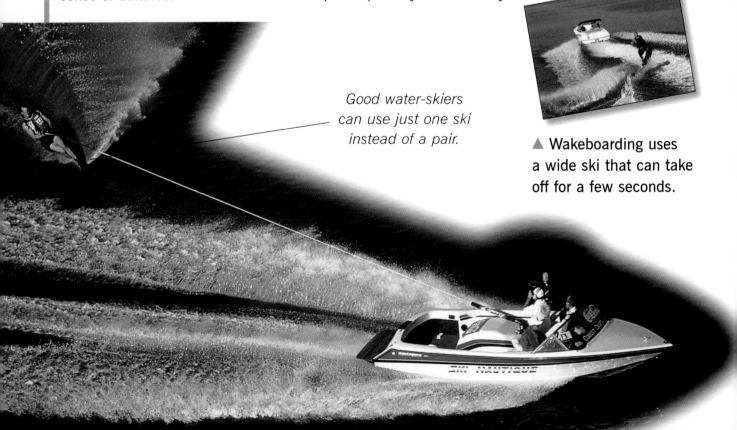

Good water-skiers can use just one ski instead of a pair.

▲ Wakeboarding uses a wide ski that can take off for a few seconds.

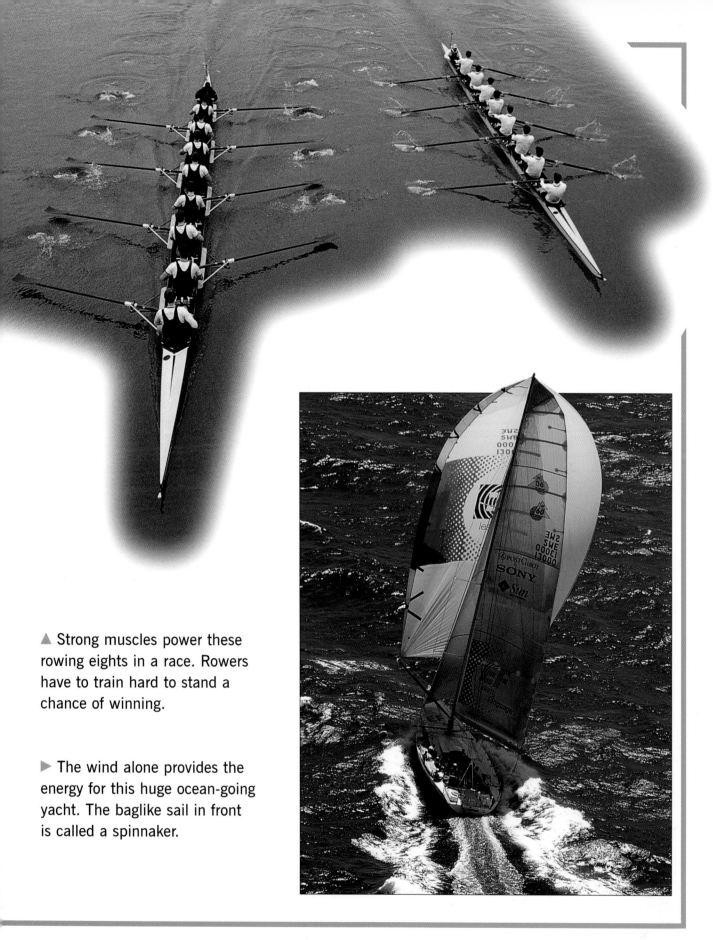

▲ Strong muscles power these rowing eights in a race. Rowers have to train hard to stand a chance of winning.

▶ The wind alone provides the energy for this huge ocean-going yacht. The baglike sail in front is called a spinnaker.

Kayaks and Canoes

Learning to use a kayak is a good introduction to water sports. But kayaking is trickier than it looks.

To a beginner, a kayak seems to have a mind of its own. It moves off easily and for a few moments all seems fine. But then the kayak goes sideways—it just won't go in a straight line!

There is a trick to steering though, and, once a kayaker learns to use the paddle correctly, a kayak becomes a very quick moving, graceful watercraft.

▲ Kayaks are a type of canoe. They can be steered accurately through white-water rapids.

▼ Safety is very important. Kayakers always wear a life jacket and a helmet. Life jackets are buoyant to help you float if you fall in the water.

helmet

life jacket

◀ This eight-year-old French girl is an expert surfer.

⛵ Waiting for the perfect wave

Some of the highest tides in the world are along the coasts of Brittany, in France.

Eager surfers may start off at low tide, with waves no more than 20 inches (50 cm) high. On the right beach though, the incoming tide soon funnels the water into huge, foaming rollers, six to ten feet high.

Then you swim out beyond the breakers to wait for the "big one," a wave that's big enough to ride all the way to shore.

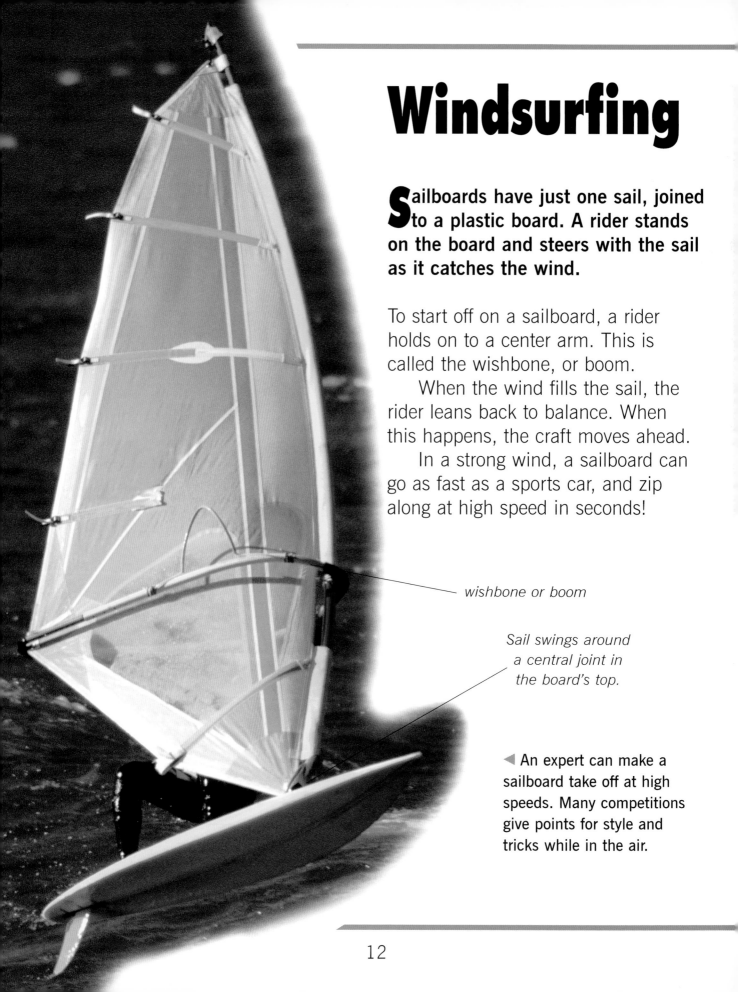

Windsurfing

Sailboards have just one sail, joined to a plastic board. A rider stands on the board and steers with the sail as it catches the wind.

To start off on a sailboard, a rider holds on to a center arm. This is called the wishbone, or boom.

When the wind fills the sail, the rider leans back to balance. When this happens, the craft moves ahead.

In a strong wind, a sailboard can go as fast as a sports car, and zip along at high speed in seconds!

wishbone or boom

Sail swings around a central joint in the board's top.

◄ An expert can make a sailboard take off at high speeds. Many competitions give points for style and tricks while in the air.

▲ Experts can take off like this. But simply zooming along can also give lots of thrills.

▼ Sailboards are made in many shapes and sizes. They all have footstraps and a slot for the sail.

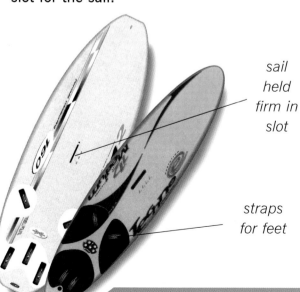

sail held firm in slot

straps for feet

 Brrr...don't get too cold!

To windsurf, you need to learn some sailing terms. You should be able to control the sail and steer the board in the water.

Learning the trick of getting your balance right takes some time. You may spend much of your first day falling into the water. This doesn't hurt, but you must not let yourself get too cold.

The moment you start to shiver, it is time to come out of the water. Then have a hot beverage and warm up.

Dinghy Sailing

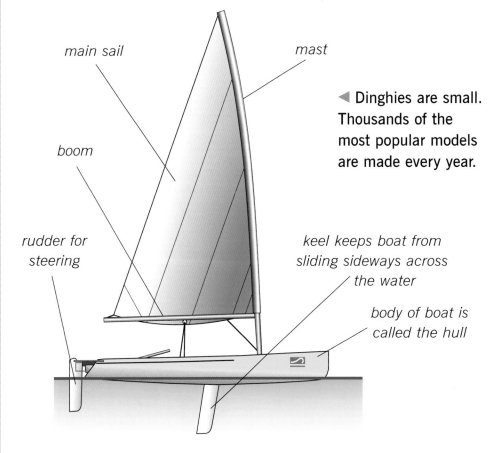

Dinghies are the smallest sailboats on the water. Most are planned for one or two crew members and have a single sail.

Dinghies are easy to launch and have sails that are simple to rig up. Before long you can be good enough to compete in races. There are many types of dinghies. The most popular type is the Laser. Over 170,000 have been made.

▲ A dinghy sailor keeps the craft level by leaning out over the water.

main sail

mast

◄ Dinghies are small. Thousands of the most popular models are made every year.

boom

rudder for steering

keel keeps boat from sliding sideways across the water

body of boat is called the hull

▶ Letters on the sails of these Laser dinghies show which countries are racing. Try to figure out those in front!

▲ This Topaz dinghy has an open-ended hull to let water drain out. The hull is packed with foam and cannot sink.

Smoother is faster

Boatbuilders are always trying to make their boats more efficient. One way is to make the hull of light and smooth plastics, instead of a traditional material like wood. A light boat can ride higher in the water, which means less drag from waves. A smooth hull cuts through the water more easily.

You can feel the difference in these materials in your own home. Try stroking a plastic plate and a wooden chopping board. You will find the plastic much smoother.

The race course is marked by these floating plastic buoys.

Ocean Racers

craft is 110 feet (33.5m) long

▲ The Club Med is one of the fastest ocean-going yachts ever built.

Huge ocean-going yachts are the queens of the seas. Many take part in long races, such as those across the Atlantic Ocean, or around the world.

The fastest ocean racers are multihull designs. Instead of just one hull, they have two (catamaran) or three (trimaran). Big multihulls are generally lighter than a traditional yacht of similar size, and they can go faster.

These racers are very big. The *Club Med* below has a mast over 131 feet (40m) high. In sea-tests, this "big cat" covered a record 626 miles (1007 km) in one day of sailing, an average of 26 miles per hour (42 kmph)!

▲ This yacht is named after a French travel company.

▲ Checking the sails on the tall mast is not a job for people scared of heights.

◀ Light but strong netting catches anyone who falls between the hulls.

Building an ocean giant

Designing and building a racing catamaran is a big job. It took 50 people nearly a year to build the twin hulls of this cat. The hulls are a sandwich of carbon-fiber, resin, and fireproof materials. This mixture is light in weight but strong enough to take the battering of ocean storms and gales.

The big cat needs a big crew during a race. It takes 14 people to sail the craft. It was built to compete in an around-the-world race, with a prize of $2 million.

The crew wears helmets and life jackets.

Motorboats

Motorboats are all about speed. They have a smooth, sleek shape to cut through the water, and powerful engines for top speeds.

Motorboats are the speed machines of the water. Even a small motorboat can usually do at least 47 mph (75 kmph). The most powerful boats can go much faster than this, at over 137 mph (220 kmph).

If you like speed, then you will love motorboats. But you have to be rich to own one. The price of the cheapest new boat is about $71,750. Bigger and faster ones can cost $717,500 or more!

▲ This is one of the fastest racing motorboats, with room for four crew in the cockpit.

▶ These single-seat racers are called hydroplanes. They skate or "plane" on the water's surface.

Like riding a boat on chunks of concrete

From a distance, a motorboat looks as if it is gliding smoothly over the water. Inside the cockpit, things are different. When speeds go over 37mph (60 kmph), a ride is very hard, and hitting a wave is like smashing into a slab of concrete.

When you ride in a motorboat, you wear a helmet, life jacket, and strap yourself in very tightly. If you don't, you may get bruised or crack a rib.

Even so, while motorboating is not a gentle sport, it is exciting and fun.

▲ Some motorboats have a catamaran design with two hulls. Air is trapped between the hulls to give the boat a smoother ride.

Jet-Ski Boats

Jet-skis are like motorbikes on water. They are driven by a powerful jet of water that squirts out of the back at high speed.

Riding a jet-ski is a real challenge. The machine bucks and bounces on the water, almost like a wild horse! It's easy to fall off, although a rider is unlikely to get hurt.

But jet-ski riders sometimes speed, go near beaches, and cause accidents with swimmers. Good riders stay away from beaches.

▲ You start off on your knees, kneeling on the jet-ski's rear platform. As speed builds up, you can get onto your feet.

Speed is controlled by a small switch on the right hand-grip.

The center bar moves up as the jet-ski gets up to speed.

◄ You can lean into turns on a jet-ski, just like cornering on a motorbike. Pushing your weight to one side helps the jet-ski dig into the water for fast, tight turns.

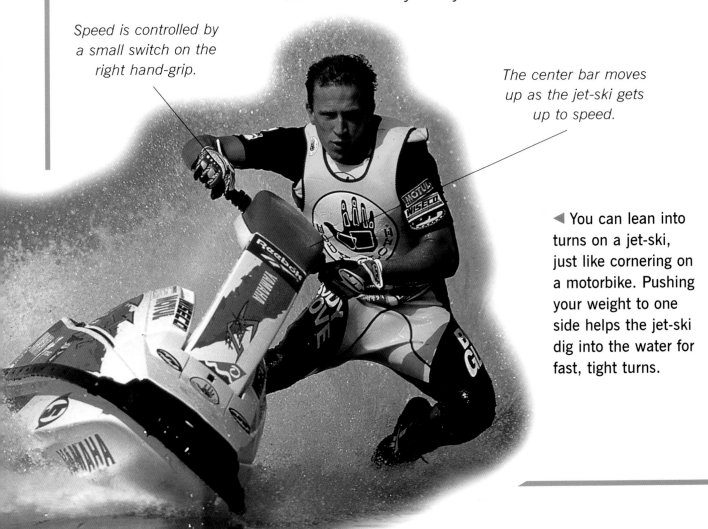

▲ Jet-ski racing is a high-speed sport, with riders
competing on a course laid out around floating markers.
Machines are fitted with specially-adjusted racing engines.

Scuba Diving

Scuba equipment makes you free to explore under the ocean. Start with a face mask and flippers, then get trained for the real thing.

You don't need to be super strong to go scuba diving, but you do need to be a good swimmer. Training usually begins with a short, "taster" session. You try on the breathing kit, then use it during a dive in a safe pool. If you're eager to learn, you can join a club and go for weekend courses. Soon you'll be ready for a real dive.

▲ Practice diving in a safe place, such as a swimming pool. Never dive alone. Scuba divers always have a diving buddy in the water.

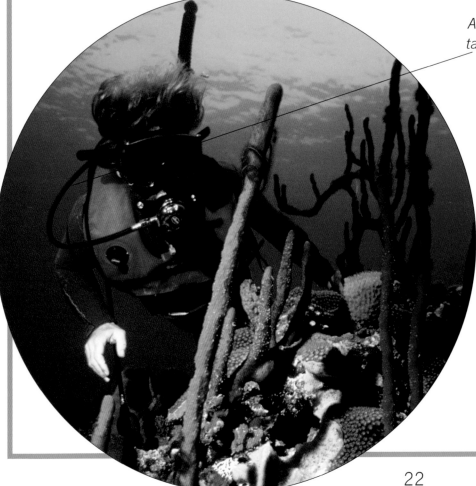

A pipe takes air from a tank to the mouthpiece

◀ Once you are trained, you can try exploring with other divers under the ocean. Perhaps you will find an old wreck, or see amazing underwater plants.

▶ This is the dream of many scuba divers —reaching out to touch a friendly dolphin!

What is scuba gear?

The word scuba stands for "self-contained underwater breathing apparatus." It links an air tank with a special mouthpiece.

The mouthpiece is an instrument that gives you air exactly when you want it. You just breathe in through your mouth, and the correct amount of air flows.

Divers may also use a suit for warmth, face mask or goggles, and a pair of rubber flippers to move quickly.

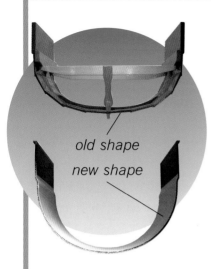

old shape

new shape

▲ Rowboats now have U-shaped hulls. These are lighter and faster than traditional wood hulls. (See top.)

New Ideas

Designers are constantly thinking up new ways to improve boats. And new water sports also appear from time to time.

Using new materials is one of the best ways to improve an old design. Few of today's boards and boats use heavy wood or metal. Instead, they are made mostly of lightweight mixtures of plastics and glues.

One new idea is combining different sports to make a new "crossover" activity. An example is kitesurfing, in which a surfboard is towed behind a kitelike wing.

▲ Kitesurfing was developed during the 1990s. Kitesurfers surf and fly short distances.

flat, sail-like mast

▲ Oars have changed shape from long and thin to short and fat. The short style gives greater speed.

◀ Trimarans are among the fastest yachts. This one has a flattened mast that acts like a tall, thin sail, for extra speed.

Hulls are joined by super-slim booms.

Water Sport Facts

Here are some facts and stories from the world of water sports.

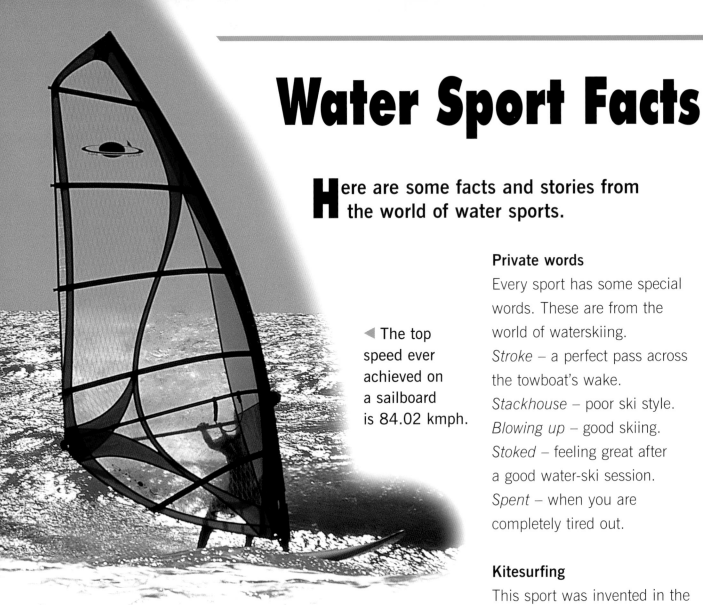

◄ The top speed ever achieved on a sailboard is 84.02 kmph.

Private words

Every sport has some special words. These are from the world of waterskiing.

Stroke – a perfect pass across the towboat's wake.

Stackhouse – poor ski style.

Blowing up – good skiing.

Stoked – feeling great after a good water-ski session.

Spent – when you are completely tired out.

Kitesurfing

This sport was invented in the 1990s and uses a large kite to pull a surfboard. The added thrill is taking off for long airborne jumps and doing stunts like spins, turns, and even flying upside down for a few seconds.

Chilly windsurfer

Dutchman Gerard-Jan Goekoop won the coldest windsurfing record in 1985, when he was ship's doctor on an Arctic research expedition.

When the ship was in pack ice near the North Pole, Goekoop put on a wet suit, then went windsurfing in the icy waters by the ship!

Long jumpers

Top water-skiers try to make record-breaking jumps off shallow ramps, that are set up to float in mid-water.

The best water-skiers can fly long distances through the air after zooming off a ramp. The women's world record water-ski jump is 172 feet (52m), the men's is 224 feet (68m).

Secret signals

Scuba divers need a way to signal underwater. They use a hand-signal system.

Scuba signs include:
Thumb up – Going up.
Thumb down – Going down.
Arm up – stop where you are.
Fist shaken from side to side – distress or emergency.

High speed kayaks

In 1995 four Hungarians paddled at 14 mph (23 kmph) over a 656 feet (200m) course.

▲ A scuba diver heads toward the seabed.

◄ Big yachts are long-haul champions of the oceans. Smaller craft are faster over short distances. The record is 53 mph (86.21 kmph) over 1,640 feet (500m), by a two-man trimaran.

A year later, a German team covered a longer 3,280 feet (1000m) course only slightly slower, at 13 mph (21 kmph).

Surfing moneymaker

U.S. surfer Kelly Slater has earned the most money from his sport. When he retired in 1998, he had made $613,194, much of it from surf-gear makers who pay him to wear their products.

Record rowing

The fastest rowing speed by one person is 10 mph (16.5 kmph), achieved in 1994, by Canadian rower Silken Laumann. Team boats are faster still—an eight-man Dutch team hit 10 mph (22 kmph) over 6,562 feet (2000m) in 1996.

Water Sport Words

▲ A family-size motorboat can also tow skiers.

Here are some technical terms used in this book.

boogie board
(BUH-gee bord)
A board that is suitable for beginners. Instead of standing up, you simply lie on your chest. Also known as a body board.

buoy (boi)
A floating marker that shows such things as a racecourse or position of rocks. Buoys are anchored by chain to the sea bottom, so they stay in place, even in strong wind or tides.

dinghy (DING-ee)
A small, open sailing boat. Dinghies usually have just one or two sails. Early types were made of wood. Modern ones are usually made of plastics.

diving buddy
(DYE-ving BUHD-ee)
One of a two-person diving team. Sport divers always go in pairs, so there is someone to help in case of emergency.

hull (huhl)
The main body of a boat or ship. Small craft may have hulls of wood or plastics. Large ships have metal hulls.

hydroplane (HYE-droh plane)
A speedboat made to skate across the water surface. Craft made with a deeper, v-shape hull cut through the water.

kayak (KYE-ak)
A type of canoe, now made of plastics. The first kayaks were made by the Inuit people of North America, who used a covering of sealskin.

keel (keel)
The bottom spine of a boat or ship. On sailboards, the keel is known as a daggerboard, and is moveable.

kitesurfing (KITE-surf-ing)
A sport in which your feet are fixed to a board, similar to a snowboard. Power comes from a large kite-like wing that tows you through the water. On windy days, high jumps and aerial stunts are possible.

life jacket (LIFE JAK-it)
A jacket that keeps your mouth and nose above the water if you fall in.

multihull
(MUHL-tee-huhl)
A seacraft with more than one hull. A catamaran has a pair of hulls, joined by booms.

◄ This water-skier wears a life jacket in case of a bad fall.

A trimaran has a center hull with outriggers on either side.

motorboat
(MOH-tur-BOTE)
A vessel built to zoom along at high speed. Power boats range from single-seaters with outboard motors to massive craft capable of 124 mph (200 kmph).

rowing eight (ROH-ing ate)
A rowboat designed for an eight-person crew. There is usually a coxswain as well, who steers the boat. Other rowboats include designs for four, two, and one person.

sandwich construction
(SAND-wich kuhn-STRUHK-shuhn)
A method of making a boat hull. It is made by building up layers of stiff carbon-fiber, mixed with resin and glue. The result is a material much lighter and stronger than wood or metal.

scuba (SKOO-buh)
Self-contained underwater breathing apparatus. An air tank is linked to a mouthpiece by a rubber pipe. Scuba gear was invented by the French explorer Jacques Cousteau, with Emil Gagnon, in 1943.

spinnaker (SPI-ni-kur)
Baglike sail used on sailing boats. Spinnakers are good for speed in light winds, and when sailing downwind.

wakeboard (WAKE-bord)
Wide board towed behind a ski-boat. On a wakeboard, you make jumps off the spray (or wake) behind the boat. You can also do rolls and stunts.

white water
(wite WAW-tur)
Name for the foaming waters in fast-flowing river sections.

wishbone
Oval-shaped handle used to control a windsurfer sail. Also known as a boom.

◀ A wakeboard, packed ready for use.

◀ A ski-boat trails a foaming wake.

Water Science

There is plenty to learn about the how-and-why of water sports and sporting machines.

▲ Jet-skis are also known as PWCs, or personal watercraft.

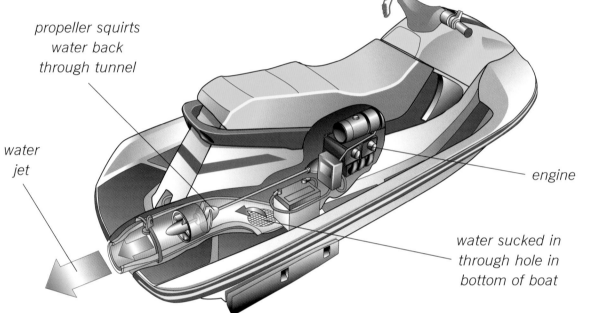

propeller squirts water back through tunnel

water jet

engine

water sucked in through hole in bottom of boat

Rocket on water

A jet-ski uses the principle of action and reaction to move. Water squirts out of the back (the action), so the jet-ski moves forward (the reaction). Try this project to see how it works.

1 Fill an empty plastic drink bottle with cold water.

2 Push a cork into the top. Fix it firmly but not tightly.

3 Lay the bottle in a bath. Push hard, and the cork will whiz out!

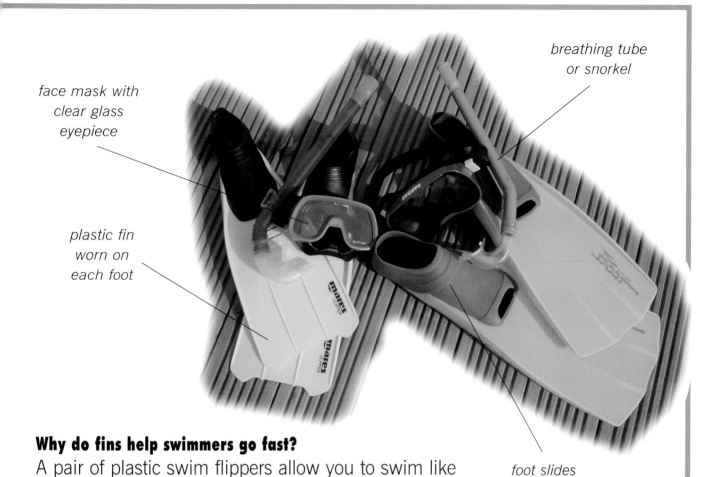

face mask with clear glass eyepiece

breathing tube or snorkel

plastic fin worn on each foot

foot slides into this part

Why do fins help swimmers go fast?

A pair of plastic swim flippers allow you to swim like a fish. The reason is that flippers increase the area of the feet, giving a swimmer more pushing power.

1 You need a small and a large paddle. We used a kitchen spatula and board.

2 Fill a bath with cold water and paddle hard with the spatula to make waves.

3 Now use the board. You will see that its extra size shifts much more water.

Index